Renegade Advisor:

How Financial Advisors Can Survive and Thrive The "Amazoning" Of Their Industry

By Dan Cuprill & Heather Stevens

RENEGADE,

Be a force to be reckoned with,
in your business and in your life.

Surround yourself with a
community of greatness,
inspiration and
like-minded rebels.

Do not sell out.

Ignore the nay-sayers.

Do not take council from
your fears.

Take bold action.

You Will Not Only Survive But Thrive.

How to Get the Most from This Book

Congratulations! You are smarter than 99% of your competition.

Most financial advisors spend morning, noon and night working in their business – booking appointments, managing client relationships, hiring (and firing) employees, and desperately trying to increase their flow of new business. However, few take the time to step back from the day-to-day to not only understand how to run their business more effectively, but also how to assess fully the threats they face.

We wrote this book for the business owners who are looking to free themselves from the daily grind and gain the freedom they dreamed of when they first opened their doors.

This book is for you if:

> ➢ You aren't making considerably more profit than you were five years ago.

> ➢ Your tired of being told the key to make more is to simply spend more.

> ➢ You're tired of wasting time with people who continuously utter the words, "I'll get back to you" and don't.

> ➢ You wish you could spend more time working "on" your business rather than "in" it.

> ➢ You worry technology is passing you and your business by. And if you are using it, will it pay off?

> ➢ You wish you could increase your level of consistently recurring revenue.

> ➢ You have lots of ideas, but struggle with how to implement them.

You're being squeezed by the industry behemoths and are starting to feel like there might not be a place for independent financial advisors anymore. All those frustrations can be eliminated, quickly and easily, by following the strategies we will outline.

There's just one thing you must do to get results – act.

You can read hundreds of marketing books and read millions of motivational sayings to pump yourself up – but that won't change anything unless you act. Don't just read this book and expect it to make a difference in your business. Knowing something is not enough. Knowing what you should do is not enough.
You must use what you see and act.

It comes down to stick-to-itive-ness.

While it may not technically be a word, it is genuine, and it is the reason why most people fail at most everything they do.

The bottom line is this: *you need to create a plan and then stick to it.* This book will help you do it.

"We are doomed."

As lifelong students of marketing, Heather and I are relatively immune to negative, fear-driven headlines like this. Many predict the world's end daily, and yet we live a life today far greater than any past generation. Back then, we had Hitler. Today, we've got Rocket Man in North Korea. Back then, we had polio. Today we have cancer. Problems come and go. But like water and a basement, we find a way to get through.

What's particularly interesting is how change forces us to adapt in an almost Darwinian way.

Consider record stores. When we were all installing car phones in the late 80's, could anyone have seen that as the beginning of the demise of the music retail business as we knew it? Highly doubtful. And yet, some records stores still exist. There aren't many, and they cater to a much smaller and different clientele. But they do live, and most likely always will. In fact, what remains today is far better than the old Sam Goody's in the mall. Check out Jerry's Records if you're ever in Pittsburgh to see what we mean.

Like many, we're avid followers of expert direct marketer Dan Kennedy's work, who has built a reputation as the millionaire-maker.

Actually, Heather borders on creepy groupie.

She owns a life-sized cut out the man.

If you don't know his work, visit www.GKIC.com.

This article, which appeared in the October 2017 edition of his NO BS newsletter, tells a disturbing tale:

Self-driving cars. Self-driving truck convoys. I won't try scaring you about using them. I know you can hardly wait. I live in an area of the country with steep hills, winding country roads, hairpin turns, roads with cliffs, flooding, snow, ice, so I harbor extreme doubts. But I won't try to scare you about any of that. Instead, let's talk about money. Henry Ford was as doubted and ridiculed when he threatened to eliminate horses and buggies from the roads with his damned-fool horseless carriages. Now, inventors and companies are racing each other to replace auto and truck drivers by substituting "autonomous vehicles."

Let's assume it all comes to be. We may see Henry Ford's historical revolution repeat itself. If it does, at a tipping point, it will accelerate, expand, and rather suddenly replace all modes of transportation utilizing humans at the controls. Its momentum is building slowly, but if and when there is ample proof the tech works and governments give a blessing, the rest will happen virtually overnight …

Ninety percent of Uber drivers removed from their gig economy incomes. Seventy percent+ of long-haul truck drivers summarily unemployed. Many who own or lease their trucks bankrupt (as Uber has done to NYC cab drivers), piling up unwanted trucks in repo lots re-sold to be re-fitted at dimes on dollars, and banks' loans behind them uncollectible. Railroads' freight volume cut by half, crashing their stock values, bankrupting most or all, and putting railroad engineers and maintenance workers on the unemployment line. City bus drivers, unemployed. If auto and truck accidents go away, the personal injury attorneys' ranks fall by half, and those remaining must step up creatively, suing more companies for more kinds of product injury claims – maybe yours – thus damaging the stock values of more and more companies, and creating mammoth consumer price inflation to cover the explosively multiplied liability and litigation costs. Hospitals: absent auto and truck accident victims, prices for remaining, fewer customers skyrocket to compensate. I'd guess at least a 25 percent rise in healthcare costs. Insurers like GEICO, Progressive, State Farm lose half their auto and truck insurance revenue. Auto body shops: fast extinct. In a 24-month time window, we could see 10-million+ jobs erased, hundreds of thousands of small businesses bankrupted, many public companies in which pension and 401k money are invested lose much of their value, triggering a Dow drop to below 10,000. Maybe 5,000. If sudden enough, triggering the next Great Depression.

Looping back to Mr. Ford, he led the second American industrial revolution, setting in motion the creation of a huge, robust, prosperous middle class and a gold-plated private sector retirement security system. However, he also set in motion a consolidation of capital and jobs into a single industry- auto manufacturing - with its orbiting ancillaries of steel, rubber and energy. When the Japanese auto invasion came, and the industry then went from domestic to global, and 80 percent of it moved offshore, the middle class that Ford invented was ravaged, shrunken and has never recovered. Our current economy is already dangerously dominated by a single industry: tech. The self-driving car and truck take the now separate auto manufacturing industry, railroad industry, public transportation industry and more and consolidate all into that single industry: tech. Ford, GM, Chrysler, etc. replaced by Apple, Google, Tesla, etc. – replacing 100 to 250 jobs with 1 to 5. Tying the entire stock market in which two-thirds of Americans are invested and one-third financially dependent on a handful of monopolistic global corporations atop one single industry. The concentration of capital is already apace; as of August, Apple has more cash in its coffers than J.P. Morgan/Chase Bank by a 20X multiple. Don't worry about bank failures for the next financial system Armageddon – worry about Apple.

Let me make three points.

VISION. As an entrepreneur, you have to force yourself to see beyond the present moment: back to historical precedents, forward to the future. You must see the potential ramifications from a single pebble dropped into a stream in a remote Asian village that emanates throughout the globe and into your business, living room, family and finances. See nothing as separated from everything. See the terrors unleashed with the opening of each new Pandora's Box, as well as the opportunities. As foreseen circumstances warrant, you must be willing to create a NEW VISION for your business. Without wholesale abandonment of what works, you have to identify THE critical and most valuable thing to invent, fix, strengthen or change.

PROACTIVITY. As an entrepreneur, you must live with a constant, pressuring demanding sense of acute urgency. Anything less is nowhere near enough. The coach and quarterback who won the Super Bowl acted as if every possession of the ball in every game all year required a score. They began scheming for each opponent, not the week before that game, but throughout the offseason. The coach is developing players for four years from now at the same time he is scheming to extend the careers of the best he has now. If you can't attend to the needs of the moment and create the future at the same time, you'll always be chasing and coping with what has already happened, making you a perennial loser.

SELF-INTEREST. No one else is ever going to care as much as you hopefully care about your interests. Any last thought that anybody in government is representing your interests should have been destroyed by the deep and systemic corruption that President Trump has laid bare. Have NO illusions. NOBODY is looking out for you. Whenever somebody says, "I'm on YOUR side," they're positioned there to reach into your pocket and steal your wallet. You have to combine Vision and Proactivity to be aggressively advancing or at least protecting your interests.

Right now, a lot of people are scared of a lot of dumb things. They have let their time and emotional well-being be usurped by social media, driven by FOMO – Fear Of Missing Out. But missing out on what? They obsess over Trump's tweets. A rising of tides, made worse anytime Gore wades his bulk into the ocean. (Tip: move inland.) Hey, let's worry about things we can do something about. I want you to be running scared, and not just on Halloween. Most of you can use the exercise. But more significantly, it's the paranoid who prosper. The business genius is never just asking: how can I grow my company? ... He's asking: If I were my company's savviest and most dangerous enemy, how would I destroy me? Of all the changing circumstances, economics, and trends, where does my greatest peril lie, that I can proactively do something about?

Which brings me to the chief subject of this month's NO BS Marketing Letter – marketing to the affluent. Several midrange restaurant chains including Chili's and Olive Garden recently announced the closing of over 100 locations by the end of 2018. This is just one of a thousand announcements of the demise of *the middle class, middle-income consumer. I began predicting this in 2004. You were warned. Now it is serious. If you are indiscriminate in choosing your customers or worse, have your business and its marketing crafted for the middle market customers, you are headed for a whale of a lot of trouble. This mandates developing a NEW AND DIFFERENT VISION FOR YOUR BUSINESS and pursuing it PROACTIVELY; aggressively and with urgency. To use a cliché, the bottom line is: You need better, higher quality, stronger, financially affluent if not outright rich customers committed to you, come hell or high water.*

 –Dan S. Kennedy

Compelling, isn't it? And frightening.

Let's throw in the fact Schwab will now manage clients' money and rebate fees. Millennials like using low-fee robo advisors. Then there's the DOL ruling that almost assures more lawsuits.

How can you, the financial advisor, develop and implement a new and different vision for your practice ahead of these changes?

Before we get into that, a little about us:

Dan Cuprill: By day, he's a financial advisor. His client base generates well over $1 million per year in assets under management fees. His firm, Matson & Cuprill, is situated in Cincinnati, OH, but works with clients in 20 states. He services all his clients using a holistic planning approach that naturally secures 100% of the client's assets. Also, Dan runs Advisor Architect, LLC, a training company dedicated to showing other financial advisors how to build a profit based practice using systems. For more information, visit www.AdvisorArchitect.com or his blog site, ProfitableAdvisor.com.

By night, Dan his is husband to Beth and father to Wes who, like his father, appreciates good wine.

Heather Stevens is not writing from a corporate ivory tower or having inherited a family business. Her methods and principles have been developed and tested through sheer pugnacious determination. She's held her own in the oil patch of Northern Alberta and became the youngest female District Manager that Lennox International had ever hired. Strapping on her pink work boots, she built a residential heating company to $1 million in sales in just 11 months, starting with a $600 van and an online classified ad.

She represents the changing face of the industry, where the biggest and best breakthroughs will be found "outside the box." The future is coming whether your business is prepared or not. You can spend the next few years worrying about your business as you become irrelevant or you can invest in developing a systematic, efficient and affordable method to compete in the new economy.

So are we doomed? Not all of us. Some will survive. And those who do will be wildly more profitable. We'll serve only clients who hire to relieve them of their financial pain and anxieties and NOT the products we sell.

To survive, we must be different. We can't just follow the status quo because the status quo will not survive the changes thrust upon it. We must be Renegades.

Chapter One:
Change the Way You Think

What would you define as a good year for your practice? Think about it? Take a few minutes and write it down.

Now, how would you define a good year for your personal life?

We're willing to bet the first one had a production goal in mind. Perhaps hitting a specific AUM target.

We hope the second answer had something to do with time. Time spent with family; time spent traveling, time spent fly fishing for king salmon (sorry...one of Dan's passions just revealed itself).

Given a choice, a good year for your practice or a good year for your life, which would you choose? Again, we hope the latter.

A few years ago, a good friend of mine decided he would transition his practice from 100% commission to 100% fee. No small task for him as he was accustomed to generating close to $1 million a year in commissions and had the lifestyle to go with it: three homes, two boats, jewelry, cars, club memberships and three employees.

As you're probably aware, annuities pay 7% commission. Assets under manage usually yield less than 1%.

I had no doubt he would succeed. He's a high energy implementer.

Almost daily he would call me with news of accounts he had landed. I could hear the passion in his voice as he crossed the production plateaus:

- $5 million
- $10 million
- $25 million
- $50 million

By year five, he exceeded $70 million of AUM. His Turnkey Asset manager loved him. He received one award after another at their annual meeting. They invited him up on stage to tell others how he did it. More impressively, he did it all with brand new clients. He didn't move a single annuity to the new fee-based structure.

With a few life insurance sales thrown in there, he was back to $1 million a year. Only this time, most of it was recurring. He no longer had to bring in new clients. Sounds great, doesn't it?

Here's the problem.

It cost him his marriage. Yes, he was having an excellent year for his business, but was the cost worth it? Could he have achieved the goal without the personal expense?

Of course, the answer is yes.

Too often, organizations who motivate and challenge us to achieve massive business success do so in a way that's completely counter to our own best interests.

Revenue goal vs. Profit Goal

From birth, advisors are taught to focus only on volume: target premium, AUM and annuity deposits.   The rationale is the more volume, the more successful an advisor will be. This standard is perpetuated further by industry awards and free trips given out to those who achieve specific sales goals.

Of course, Business 101 teaches sales are meaningless if they don't lead to profit. And yet, our industry never discusses profit. An advisor who prioritizes profit over growth is labeled a "small thinker."

Gold Watch, Custom Shirts, and No Money

I'll admit it...I'm frugal. Don't get me wrong, I spend my money, but only on things with undeniable value.

I once shared a hotel room with a friend at an industry meeting (as I said, I'm frugal). Great guy. A commission-based advisor who wanted to move more money into AUM. Or so he said.

I learned a lot about him that week. He had owned a handful of Corvettes, liked to have his shirts custom made and wore mostly Rolex watches.

Very goal driven, he was proud of having achieved "All-Star" status with his FMO for annuity production. But something bugged him.

He was broke. Sure, he'd earned a lot, but he spent a lot. To generate the revenue that made him an all-star, he was required to spend a significant portion of it. And while he had a very comfortable lifestyle, he was always one bad quarter away from losing most of it.

Here was a "financial advisor" failing to live the very advice he gave to his clients: Live within your means and save a percentage of your earnings.

So, I asked, "What makes it a good year for you?"

"At least $10 million of annuity production."

"This is why you're broke," I explained.

"For your entire career, your so-called partners have told you (your FMO, your Broker-Dealer,

Your TAMP) that it's all about hitting a production goal. Do whatever it takes to hit those numbers, even if it means pulling money from your IRA or getting another credit card. Am I right?"

"That's what they say."

"I know. I even had one tell me that money invested in my business is worth far more than money invested in my portfolio."

"Yup," he said. "I've heard that one, too. In fact, it was by a guy who coaches other advisors. He argued it was better spent on his coaching system."

"Of course. They perpetuate this myth that there's a lottery out there ready to be won. Rather than encourage steady, consistent growth in your profits, they tell you to think big, get in the fast lane, and become an overnight success. Just keep spending money to make money. Drop tons of direct mail for dinner seminars, get a radio show or a TV show. Rent a high-end office. Hire a large staff. If you're not spending at least 60% of your revenue on your business, you'll never make it. Am I right?"

"Sounds like you were at that meeting," he laughed.

"I was, but I never took their advice. Early in my career, I recognized what was often in the best interest of our product vendors ran counter to my own."

It may seem incredibly obvious, but the goal of any business is NOT to hit a revenue goal. Instead, its purpose is to reach a PROFIT goal. You'll never hear that discussed in any vendor meeting. In fact, I've heard some discourage focus on profit. "Focus on growth and profit takes care of itself."

Tell it to Uber.

We know how vendors make money: new business. While TAMPS do earn recurring revenue on AUM, their staff is usually bonused on the "net new" assets their advisors bring in. They understand advisors can come and go, taking their accounts with them. So, the push is always to keep hitting a new AUM goal: $50 million, $100 million, $1 billion.

We love big goals, but only when they translate into more personal net worth and free time. More on that shortly.

Let's now go back to the second question I asked earlier: What makes an excellent year for your personal life?

Does hitting high production goals translate into more free time to enjoy your life? Have you ever met a large producer who filed for bankruptcy? We have. He won every award possible, but couldn't pay his mortgage. His personal life was a wreck.

Revenue doesn't give you freedom, no matter what the vendors say.

Profit gives you freedom. Profit is money with no strings attached because you already earned it. Profit wisely invested grows without any effort on your part. Focus on profit over revenue and the entire outlook on your business will change.

Contrary to what your vendors will tell you, $500,000 in revenue that produces $350,000 in profit is a better business than one generating $1,000,000 and netting $500,000.

Practice A: Paul the Producer

Paul's practice generates about $1 million a year with 60% coming from one-time commission-based products (life insurance and annuities) and $400,000 from AUM. Paul directly manages money for about 200 families. To service this business, he has a full-time office manager, a marketing assistant, a first impressions coordinator, and a client service manager. He typically spends $200,000 a year in marketing. Staff salaries and office overhead run about $300,000. So, Paul bring homes home 500,000 (50%).

Practice B: Roberta the Renegade

Roberta has 100 fee based clients averaging about $4,000 a year per in AUM fees. She charges all new clients a one-time planning fee of $1,500 and assists fully with implementing her recommendations. This includes providing products like long-term care, life insurance, and disability insurance in addition to portfolio management which she completes with the help of a turnkey asset manager. She spends about $50,000 a year to grow her business through a variety of workshops and social media efforts. She pays one staff person $50,000 a year. Her remaining fixed overhead runs about $50,000.

Last year commission from insurance reached $100,000, giving her total revenue of $500,000. This allowed her to pocket 350,0000 (70%).

Traditional thinking says Practice A (Paul's) is a healthier business because he generates more revenue and take-home pay. Paul gets trophies at his FMO meetings. Roberta is lucky to get a free lunch. In fact, she's routinely encouraged by her vendors to "think big," "get in the fast lane," and spend more money to make more money. In other words, to be more like Paul.

Ironically, it is Paul who should learn from Roberta. Her business is the superior practice. In fact, it isn't even close.

Think about it:

Which one of these advisors do you think spends more time with family?

Which one has fewer staff headaches?

Which one must deal with employees quitting or their sick children?

Which one must pay more for benefits and payroll taxes?

Which one is better prepared to handle a drop off in new clients?

Which one has more freedom?

Which one do you think invests more money every year?

Which one do you think hits the credit line more often?

Roberta would never trade places with Paul for the extra $150,000. In fact, she could generate that additional $150,000 with far less effort using her existing model that produces a 70% profit margin. Here average AUM client is considerably larger than Paul's not because she targets the super wealthy, but because of her holistic sales and planning approach. As a rule, she works only with clients willing to let her manage 100% of their money. Not only does this make more sense from a profitability perspective, she feels strongly it's in the client's best interest to have a uniform investment strategy. As she likes to tell them, "Having two advisors is a lot like have two heart surgeons operate at the same time. They both get paid, but the patient will probably die."

Paul, on the other hand, is willing to take whatever business a client will give him. He also doesn't charge a planning fee out of fear they'll reject him before he can sell them a product.

Even when Paul has a good year, he must keep a lot of the excess profit in cash to protect himself against a down quarter since his fixed overhead is so high.

Paul begins each year setting a revenue goal.

Roberta begins each year setting a profit goal.

Renegade Advisors like Roberta judge a year not by the revenue they've produced but by things like profit margin, additions to their net worth and personal freedom. Despite receiving less in cash, Roberta's business is more valuable should she wish to sell it considering her average client is larger, and her overhead is lower.

Think Profit, Not Production

Interestingly enough, Paul can create more profit by doing less, not more. He simply needs to ignore his vendors' advice.

Like my friend earlier, Paul has been told the key to success is to spend money on marketing, even if he doesn't have it. He should use direct mail to conduct a lot of dinner seminars. He needs an elaborate office with a large staff. This type of advice serves the vendor well, but not Paul. High overhead forces him to keep selling commission based products and ignoring long term profitability and equity value in his businesses. Perhaps unintentionally, one vendor demonstrates this conflict of interest in a book called <u>The Advisor Breakthrough</u> by Shawn Sparks.

"I make a good deal of money," one producer like Paul told us at a vendor meeting. "But I have to spend a lot to do it. I'd really like to slow down, but I don't know how. The beast has to be fed."

"You're running a sales center," we explained. "Wouldn't you rather own a profit center? If you created the beast, you can kill it."

Changing His Thinking Pattern

We've worked with a lot of Pauls over the years. They are typically high achievers who are driven somewhat by competition. Knowing this, vendors create all kinds of incentives built around production goals.

A better approach is to first determine the life and practice you want and then work backwards to build it.

> ➢ What kind of clients do you want?
> ➢ What hours would you like to work?
> ➢ What kind of work do you want to never do?

Simple as it may sound, these visions serve as powerful guides as you make decisions.

Still, it's a numbers business. We get that. So, let's begin with another end goal: profit.

How much profit do you need to have a comfortable lifestyle, do the things you want to do, spend free time the way you want it, and invest money for your future? Let's assume for Paul it is $500,000. He sees himself as a success and doesn't want to retreat. His $400,000 in AUM fees is automatic. He could fire all his people and work from home and still have $400,000 arriving every year.

At the moment, he's also generating another $600,000 in commission revenue. But since it's not recurring, he collects it only if he keeps his sales center open. Of that additonal $600,000, he's really keeping only $100,000 for himself. That's a payout of only 16%. The rest goes ot the overhead needed to create it.

Is all that effort worth it for just a 16% return, or could the extra $100,000 in profit be acquired in a more efficient manner?

True, Paul can never really escape some overhead, but he can reduce it, and in the process, raise his profitabilty.

Can three people do the work of four? Can two do the work of three?

Can a smaller office of simlar quality be had for less rent?

Could using a turn key asset manager reduce the daily workload, requiring less staff and time?

In almost every case, we find staff is added NOT because the owner completed a thorough analysis of what his business needed to maximize profit. Instead, we usually hear answers like this when we ask how an advisor built his staffing model:

➤ Well, we needed someone more proficient with computers. So, I hired someone.

➤ Angie's parents are one of my clients. She was a marketing major at Central Northwest Tech. They're a good marketing school, so I figured she could help with my growth.

➤ Well, Billy was out with knee surgery, I hired Ben to fill in. Ben did such a good job in Billy's absence; I decided to keep them both.

➤ Rick was having a hard time with the workload, so I decided to get him some help.

The first employee you hire brings you a solid return in almost every case we've studied. Still, we know advisors who go the opposite way and personally complete every task in their office, from paperwork to running seminars. It robs them of free time and a life.

One staff person per every 200 clients makes a lot of sense. Even two might work. Three or four? We're skeptical. If the ambition of the business is to achieve a profit goal, overhead (mainly salaries) must be heavily scrutinized. Here's how the Renegade Advisor deals with staffing needs:

> ➢ Need someone good with computers? Either train your current staff member or replace him/her with someone who is. Yes, fire that person because he/she no longer has the necessary skills to do the job.

> ➢ Never hire your clients' children. Firing them is incredibly difficult. Same with family members. We don't care if they went to Harvard or worked with Eugene Fama. Few things are less valuable to a business than a college degree. It's merely a qualifier. Now, if she had a track record for generating

new clients, then you can consider it. But even then, we recommend you do it on a freelance basis.

➢ Consider yourself to be a basketball team. A roster has just 12 players. If one goes on the DL, someone can be signed to replace. But once the injured player returns, someone must go.

➢ Maybe Rick should be replaced with someone who can keep up with the workload. It should at least be considered.

Unless you can quantify bringing on new people translates into profit, don't.

Renegade Rule: Profit is Predictable

Renegade Advisors manage their years not by striving to meet a production goal, but by working to ensure a profit goal.

Step One: Create an operating budget. Every successful business forecasts the following year's revenue and expenses. Managers are held accountable for meeting them.

Step Two: Keep in your business only the amount of money needed to run it. This means every time you get paid, a percentage of that check immediately leaves the business account and is transferred to your brokerage account.

Step Three: Never spend more than what's in the business account. If there isn't enough to buy "the next great thing," you don't buy it.

Then Don't Take the Trip

Vendors love to host meetings. Every year I'm invited to at least a dozen. The FMO's "Game Changer Meeting." The Turnkey Asset Manager's "Total Transformation Meeting." The Business Coaches, "Complete Makeover Meeting." Each meeting has a theme, and each session promises to give you the secrets to achieving a record year. Full disclosure: I've been known to host a few myself.

I once got a call from an advisor asking if he should spend $2,000 to attend one of them.

"Do you go every year?" I asked.

"Yes."

"Anything dramatically changes year to year?"

"No, but it's a good way to network with other advisors."

"When you say network, what do you mean?"

"It's a community type of thing. I guess it's mostly social."

"If you don't attend the meeting, can you still get information on what you may have missed?"

"Oh yeah, they mail out a full package of materials including video of the best presentations."

"Do you see any way this meeting will add to your profitability this year?"

"No."

"Then don't take the trip."

We're not against education. Far from it, but a profit-driven mindset doesn't just fly across the country because there's money in the bank to pay for it. To the contrary, regularly attended meetings can become a waste of time and money, especially if you receive the information in other ways. They also rob you of time.

Every expense should be evaluated three ways:

1. Is it consistent with my vision?
2. Will it bring me a recognizable return?
3. Can I obtain the benefit in other ways?

Vendor meetings are principally sales meetings designed to get you motivated to sell. The enthusiasm generated is rarely long lasting which is why the subject matter rarely changes from year to year. In fact, they are directed not at the longtime attendee but the newcomer.

Focusing on a profit vs. revenue goal allows you to make decisions like this one much more quickly. Spending $2,000 on travel will require $200,000 in new assets under management to break even profit wise. If the same information can be had for less, the decision is an easy one.

Key Take Away Points:

1. Establish the business you want and then work backwards.
2. Your goal should be to hit a profit goal, not a revenue goal.
3. You won't achieve profit accidentally. It requires the establishment and adherence to a budget.
4. Before spending any money, ask yourself three questions:
    a. Is it essential to the running of my business?
    b. Will it bring me a recognizable return?
    c. Can I obtain the benefit in other ways?

Chapter Two:

Change the Way You Market

Many financial advisors believe they have a marketing problem.

And they do – but not in the way they may believe.

As a financial advisor, you've likely been an advertising victim. You're not sure what works and what doesn't, but you're hesitant to stop what *might* be working. You're always on the lookout for the next new strategy or tactic. For most advisors, when a salesperson appears and starts to talk about that next bright, shiny new thing (Facebook), out come the checkbooks, despite still not knowing whether the marketing is going to work.

The real marketing problem so many advisors suffer from is not a lack of website traffic or brand building – but rather trying to achieve success by repeating the same mistakes and over again.

But there is a solution.

To escape this, you must have a reliable, predictable, consistent SYSTEM that will efficiently and affordably provide high quality leads that convert efficiently into clients. By high quality, we refer to people who have more money than your average client, want you to manage it all, and will stay with you through up and down markets.

Even If You Think You're Keeping Up, You're Falling Behind...

Many advisors today try to incorporate some technology into their marketing – they have a website, maybe even a Facebook page. They might <u>even</u> allow clients to book appointments online!

The digital landscape is changing, and there's more opportunity than ever before... however, most independent advisors we meet are realistically 5 – 10 years behind the times.

Even those who try to keep up are finding that platforms are integrating and rolling out new features regularly. New "niche" services are popping up, promising results-as-if-by-magic and investors are becoming more and more sophisticated in their ability to research the industry, and your company.

You're Unique, Just Like Everybody Else...

If you are currently using platitudes or generic statements in your marketing such as "Family Owned," "Industry Leader Since..." or "In Business Since...," you likely have a marketing problem.

When you try to speak to "everyone" with general, broad stroke comments, no one listens. The days of generic messaging and brochure-type websites being effective are virtually gone (for those that are focused on growing their business).

You need to "humanize" your company as well as provide information that's relevant to your prospects while offering much, much less about you. This can be challenging for any business, as they love to talk about how they are different, however...you'll sound just like Charlie Brown's teacher – no one listens.

People do business with those they know, like and trust – not a corporate logo or brand, especially when it comes to making decisions about their financial future.

It's not that acknowledging your years in business isn't important, it's simply that there's a time and place for everything – and leading with it is not the time or the place.

The majority of people scan information with a "WIIFM" mentality – *what's in it for me*?

Your best strategy is to address that right from the beginning.

Being in the Right Place at the Right Time

In his book, *The Ultimate Sales Machine*, the late Chet Homes talks about only 3% of a given market at any given time are ready to buy. These people are looking for your services and ready to act *right now*.

This group is where most advisors focus their efforts!

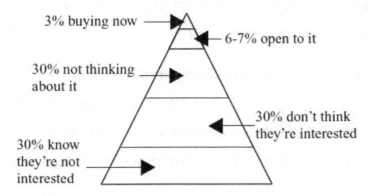

But there's a large percentage of the market that is preparing to make decisions in the next 3 – 9 months, which is being largely ignored.

Here's where you educate your market and become their partner, not just another advisor for them to information shop...

The beauty of education-based marketing is it appeals even to those who are "not interested at the moment" because it grabs their attention.

This requires a long-term, bigger picture type vision that not all businesses are willing to dedicate resources to, leaving it wide open for you.

Getting Leads

How many times have you asked yourself, *"If I'm paying for all this advertising...where are all my leads??"*

Are you tired of paying for ads...that don't seem to perform?

Whether your current advertising consists of direct mail, seminars, radio, Google AdWords or Social Media, every marketing company is trying to sell you more traffic to your website.

But there's something you must know:

"You don't have a traffic problem."

Traditional marketing relies on TV, radio, flyers, trade shows, pay-per-click, organic search results or even social media to drive prospects to either call your office or visit your website with the single goal of booking an appointment. You see, all your marketing money is aimed at bringing people to your website – but 85% of them aren't ready to book an appointment (no matter how hard you bribe them!) They're looking for answers without having to talk to a salesperson.

This means that the real problem is the lack of a system that maximizes traffic – and for most advisors, this means over 50% of their advertising budget could be be flushed down the toilet.

The truth is, most businesses don't get anywhere near the sales they could be getting, or should be getting from their existing marketing budget. And more than likely, your business is no exception.

If you've been an advisor for more than 20 years, you reminisce about the "good ole days." Back then, seminar marketing was somewhat new, and the internet was in its infancy, as was 24-hour financial news. Pension plans were being replaced by 401k's, and baby boomers had yet to retire. It was the golden era of financial advice. Lots of people needed it and had nowhere to turn.

That invitation to pay $49 to attend a three-night workshop was like manna from heaven. Advisors booked 50 couples a night easily for these seminars. After three weeks, the attendees felt they knew you and couldn't wait to hire you.

Then came "dinner seminars." Who could resist a night of free food and financial advice? Few did. Advisors packed rooms at will.

Of course, like everything, the enthusiasm subsided.

Numbers started to fall. Lots of dinner seminar attendees showed no interest in working with the advisor, leading to the name "plate lickers."

In markets like Fort Lauderdale, a person can now get a free meal almost every night, courtesy of a local "financial advisor."

While these seminars still work in some markets, others have apparently reached a saturation point that requires the profit-driven advisor to adopt a different strategy to be profitable.

One Time vs. Recurring Revenue

Your marketing approach should be influenced by how you're compensated.

Commission-based advisors can spend $10,000 on a dinner seminar with the expectation of landing just one client willing to put $500,000 in an annuity.

$500,000 x 7% commission = $35,000.

$35,000 - $10,000 mail and food cost = $25,000

For the fee-based advisor earning 1% a year, break even doesn't even occur until year two. This difference explains why annuity FMO's push dinner seminars heavily. The math works in their favor.

Mailing out 10,000 invitations to people who don't know you is a lot like hunting for deer blindfolded with a machine gun. You might find your target, but you'll waste a lot of ammo along the way.

Rather than mail out 10,000 pieces with the hope 30 will attend, wouldn't it be great if you knew who those 30 were in advance?

Of course,... but can you?

In a way, you can.

Twenty-five years ago, Dan Kennedy first published his system, Magnetic Marketing. In it, he made a distinction between brand advertising and direct marketing.

Here's an excellent example of brand marketing:

Now, direct marketing:

See the difference?

The first ad has a powerful image, but it does
absolutely nothing to motive the prospect to
act. Is the reader supposed to be so inspired by
a geyser that he gets in his car and runs to Bank
of America? No doubt the ad firm is proud of

this ad, but there is no way to quantify its success.

By contrast, the second ad does everything the first one doesn't. It tells a powerful story AND provides clear instructions on what to do next.

While we're paying homage to Mr. Kennedy, here are his 10 Rules for Marketing as paraphrased by Darcy Juarez. To see the original, visit https://gkic.com/blog/direct-response-marketing-2/10-direct-marketing-rules/

Rule One: There Will Always Be an Offer or Offer(s)

"Nothing, I mean nothing, goes out your door without offers."

To generate a response from your consumers, you need an irresistible offer that is going to motivate them to take act **IMMEDIATELY.** What will you offer them? Is it going to be of value to them? How will it improve their current situation? Ask yourself these questions, and **NEVER** end a 'conversation' with your audience without making the offer.

Dan says you'll find a lot of businesses get by with 'implied offers.' They'll give all their details but won't **ACTUALLY** say what it is they'll do for you.

But what **REALLY** generates a response is direct marketing that tells the consumer how your product can enhance their life, solve their problems, make their day better, etc., and the steps they need to take to reap the benefits.

This is how you make money!

Rule Two: There Needs to Be a Reason to Respond Right Now

If you're unfamiliar with direct-response copywriter **John Carlton,** I recommend you get familiar right now. A friend of Dan's, John advises imagining your prospective customer as a gigantic sloth, unlikely to move, with its phone out of reach.

You need to think about this sloth when constructing your offer. Is a plain, mediocre offer going to cause that sloth to move, reach out for its phone and act? *Probably not.*

Your offer should generate a direct response. That's the whole point. I reiterate my point about providing value to your prospects - if you can honestly convince them that investing in your product/service will answer their prayers and satisfy their current desires, then you're onto a winner.

Rule Three: Always Give Clear Instructions

I'd like to turn your attention to Dan's two sub-rules:

- **Confused consumers do nothing**

- **Most people can follow directions**

Anything you put together in your next strategy, whether it's a flier, an ad, a sales letter, etc., make sure the pathway to acting is clear for the consumer…. "with high sidewalls (to prevent the prospect from wandering off)."

If you're currently sending materials **WITHOUT** clear instructions, STOP. Make some changes.

Rule Four: There Will Be Tracking and Measurement

Dan says; *"you need real, hard facts and data to make good, intelligent marketing decisions."*

Do you want to make unintelligent marketing decisions?

Didn't think so...

When making marketing decisions, it doesn't matter what you and your colleagues think/feel, etc. It matters what your AUDIENCE thinks and feels.

"Tracking means accurately collecting all the information you need to determine which advertising is working and which isn't, which offer is pulling and which isn't, what kind of marketing has traction and what doesn't."

Ultimately, you'll be able to know what your ROI is for each dollar. If you get systems in place to capture all the data you need, and make the time to get a thorough analysis underway, then what seems like a confusing drag will start to become profitable and easier the more you do it... especially if your employees tend to become lazy with or confused by the whole concept.

"From now on, you shall spend no dollar without tracking ROI."

Rule Five: Branding as By-Product

If you're the CEO of a giant company that is recognized worldwide, then, by all means, invest in brand identity. If you're an entrepreneur investing your own capital, then take Dan's advice - *"focus on response and sales."*

Sure, you may actually build your brand without knowing along the way, which is awesome. But don't spend time doing it on purpose. Dan states there are many types of direct response ads that are designed to motivate qualified leads to step forward and take action, which succeed **WITHOUT** branding.

Rule Six: There Will Be Follow-Up

There are fortunes in the follow-up. Most marketers make the mistake of only following up with a lead on ONE occasion.

But to be a **SMART** marketer, you need to build out a way to continue this follow-up with your prospects.

Imagine somebody refers you to one of their closest friends. Or a business fellow, perhaps. What are you going to do? Simply say 'thanks' and move on?

NO NO NO!

You speak with the person who made the referral, and you ask them for their closest friend or business fellow's details, so you can approach them personally. Start up a sequence that involves a letter or email, with something free and valuable that is going to kickstart this new relationship.

No response? Send another letter or email. Keep at it!

Rule Seven: There Will Be Strong Copy

I love this quote from Dan: *"You can't send a shy, timid Casper Milktoast guy out into the street to knock on a door of a home or walk into a business and begin nearly a whisper for a few minutes of the prospect's time. So you can't do that with an ad, flier, letter or postcard either. Send Arnold Schwarzenegger instead."*

In a nutshell, your copy must be compelling enough to get your prospects to take immediate action. Your vocabulary choices should aggravate your prospect's problems so much so that they can almost **FEEL** the pain, and then soothe them immediately with whatever it is you're offering, and how it can solve their issue.

Think about your audience. Speak to them like they're human beings (which they are...) in a conversational tone that hooks them in with power words, packs a punch and sticks in their mind.

(NOTE: For further information on kick-ass sales copy, I urge you to read another of Dan's books, *The Ultimate Sales Letter*.)

Rule Eight: In General, It Will Look Like Mail-Order Advertising.

Dan says that 'father of advertising' David Ogilvy once admitted: *"Only direct-response guys really know what they are doing"* and that **HIS** guys were guessing. Who would you copy?

The 'G' in GKIC, Bill Glazer, is a 'master' at using mail-order style advertising. Our two founders suggest making a swipe file of mail-order newspapers and magazine advertisements that show clear calls to action. Next time you construct an offer, flip through the file for inspiration.

Rule Nine: Results Rule, Period.

From this moment forth, you are (if not already) completely, wholly, ultimately results-driven.

Nobody **EXCEPT** your customers is going to put money into your business and personal bank account. NOBODY ELSE. All that matters is what your customers think. If you make sales, then your strategy has worked. If it doesn't make sales, scrap it.

Rule Ten: You Will Be a Tough-Minded Disciplinarian and Keep Your Business on A

Strict DIRECT Marketing Diet For At Least Six Months

Is there room for doing workshops if you follow these rules? Of course. But rather than invite just anyone, you'll need to take a more pointed approach than mass mailing to strangers.

How I Build My Mailing List

Call any direct list vendor, and they'll sell you a list based on a wide variety of factors: age, address, homeowner, investable assets, eye color (okay, I made that one up). The list is extensive and who knows how they gather it. Here's one thing you won't find on their list: what keeps them up at night.

Using Kennedy's rules, my firm builds its own mailing list magnetically by promoting not our events to the public, but our Retirement Rescue Toolkit.

The kit offers information on how to have a tax-free retirement. It contains a book, a free report, an audio CD, and DVD, and letter that makes a very special and limited time offer.

Once people are delivered the kit, they receive a number of follow-ups, including emails, a print newsletter, a podcast, a webinar, and invitations to our upcoming events. If someone orders a kit, there's an almost 10% chance he or she will attend one of our live events within the next 12 months.

It costs less than $10 to send a Retirement Rescue Toolkit. We typically spend $500 per month promoting it on social media.

Far more cost effective.

It takes time to build a list, which is why I don't recommend advisors abandon direct mass mail until they've built their list to where it's large enough to be self-supporting.

Key Take Away Points:

1. Effective marketing is built around sending the right message to the right market using the right form of media.

2. All forms of media work if you follow the ten rules.

3. A tangible lead magnet is a highly efficient way to build a list of prospects who respond to your message.

Chapter Three:
Change the Way You Sell

Back to the good old days.

In those days, selling was largely order taking. Salespeople armed with company cars drove from one account to another filling supply orders. There was no actual selling going on. Mostly relationship management.

The salesperson was the supply chain. The only way you could get the product was the salesperson. That's no longer the case.

The salesperson today is rarely needed to buy the product. In fact, skipping the salesperson altogether is, for many, the preferred method. Have you ever seen something in a store and then order it online? I've bought my last two cars this way.

Too many advisors fail to understand this. They think it's about the product, so much so they will not only market the product, they'll accept clients who care just about the product.

"I Need to Roll a CD"

Because we do a fair amount of marketing, we get a lot of calls.

Caller: I'd like to talk to someone about rolling a CD.

Dan: Great. Do you mind if I ask a few questions?

Caller: No problem. Go ahead.

Dan: Can I ask why you feel you should roll the CD, as you put it?

Caller: Well, it's paying only 1%, and I think I should do better.

Dan: I understand. Is this money you expect to use in the short run, say less than five years?

Caller: Probably.

Dan: Okay...in that case, does it make sense to put the money at risk at all?

Caller: Well, I'd just like to see what you have.

Dan: I understand. Have you looked online at all or done any research?

Call: Yes, in fact, I've got a list of funds from Morningstar that interest me.

Dan: Great. Have you contacted them to see how you can invest directly with them?

Caller: No, not yet. Again, I was hoping to see what you might suggest.

Dan: Sure, I appreciate that. Have you spoken to other financial advisors?

Caller: I have. In fact, I have an appointment with Edward Jones tomorrow.

Dan: Great, good firm. Can I offer some advice?

Caller: Yes! Please do.

Dan: Sound like you already have a pretty good idea what you want to do. My advice is just to call the funds you like and ask them to send you paperwork.

Caller: But I'd like to see what you might suggest.

Dan: I doubt they'd be any better. I think you've got this.

Be honest, would you have handled this call the same way? Most advisors I know would not. They'd see it as a quick and easy sale. Within 24 hours, they'd have the person in their office looking at brochures and illustrations.

Of course, this sale is anything but easy. In fact, it's almost certain to end with the prospect saying, "Thanks, I'll be in touch." And of course, he won't be in touch. You'll never hear from him ever again.

This prospect knew very well an advisor isn't needed to buy a mutual fund. So, he did his research, but since he's not an expert, he decides to pick the brain of one.

But this one (me) wasn't willing to play ball.

This is what I call a "logic-driven" prospect.

He wants a product. Nothing else. Your relationship with him will be based solely on whether or not you have a product he wants but cannot get any other way. And that product better perform in the short run. If it doesn't, he'll pull up stakes and head out to the next product vendor.

You have (or had) clients like this. Are they the ones on which you'd like to build your practice?

I hope not. They are parasites who will suck the life blood from you. When the phone rings, you'll cringe out of fear it's them. They'll continuously require you to justify your fee. They'll also complain your fee is too high. Chances are they won't let you manage all their money, but they'll take full advantage of your time and resources.

In the past, they've had multiple advisors, or they've managed their own money. They have strong opinions about personal finance and will often challenge your ideas. Even if you think you have all their money, you don't. They have an account on the side. Or with another advisor.

Even if they have millions to invest, the Renegade Advisors sees them as less than ideal and very nicely says, "I don't think you need my help."

"I Can't Sleep at Night"

Phil and Karen had every reason to believe their retirement would be fantastic. A retired dentist, he'd accumulated an impressive portfolio that should easily last their lifetime and still leave money for their kids.

Dan: So, what would make this a good meeting?

Phil: For you to show me how to alleviate the stress I have about money.

Dan: Can you tell me more?

Karen: He doesn't sleep. He worries about money all the time.

Dan: Interesting. Can you be a little more specific?

Phil: I know compared to most people I should feel good. It's a decent nest egg. But if things don't work out, I can't exactly go back to being a dentist. On the other hand, I refuse to just give my money to an insurance company for a low annual payment. I want us to have a comfortable retirement and leave money to our kids. But every time I pick up the paper, I worry. It seems like there's always a crisis. This stuff didn't' bother me when I was working, but now all I do is watch the news.

Dan: What have you done to address it so far?

Karen: We had an advisor, but we didn't care for him. He never called and didn't seem interested in us.

Dan: So you no longer work with him?

Karen: No. We've been doing it ourselves for the past year.

Dan: How is that going?

Phil: I hate it. I don't know what I'm doing. Look, I realize I'm smart enough to figure this all out, but I just don't want to.

Dan: I understand. Would you like for me to explain to you how we help people who, like you, have some anxiety about their money?

Phil: Yes, please. That's why we're here.

What's the main difference between the caller and Phil/Karen?

It is the absence and presence of emotion. Or to use a David Sandler term, pain.

The evidence is overwhelming that people make buying decisions based not on logic but emotion.

The best clients have hired you not because of the funds or insurance products you sold but because they were insecure about their financial future and needed help. They were filled with some level of anxiety and wanted you to alleviate it.

Those are your ideal clients. Those are the clients likely to hire you for life regardless of what markets do.

So, why would you ever take on any other type of client?

Seems obvious, and yet, time and again advisors bring on clients they know deep down are not a good fit. As soon as markets take a tumble, they are reminded as to why.

Many qualities can make a prospect ideal, but the presence of anxiety or pain trumps all. Without it, you should never offer your services. Evaluate your prospects based not on what you perceive their concerns should be. Do it based on what they tell you.

Think like an endodontist.

Thanks mostly to good genes, I had no idea what an endodontist was until I started biting lifesavers. For those of you with good teeth, endodontists perform root canals. It is the perfect profession.

For one, they work only with people in pain. Serious pain.

Second, the people know the endodontist can end the pain in minutes.

Three, the price is no object.

Now, imagine if someone showed up at the endodontist and did not need a root canal. Instead, he was just there to find out what the doctor did in case he should need one in the future. Absurd, right? I'm sure the doctor would think so.

And yet, financial advisors let tire kickers in their office all the time.

"I'm doing great, financially, but I'd like to get a second opinion."

How many people ask a doctor for a second opinion after receiving a clean bill of health?

"Gee doc. My doctor says I'll live to 106, but I want a second opinion."

I'll ask for a second opinion if you want to crack open my chest. Otherwise, I'll take the doctor's word that I'm fine.

Those seeking a second opinion are like the earlier caller. They want free advice. The Renegade Advisor won't give it to them...ever. He knows it's a waste of time and money.

Like a good endodontist, the Renegade Advisor spends time only with those who genuinely need help.

Don't Try to Make them "Sick"

While most advisors with whom we counsel understand the need for "pain" before establishing a client relationship, some are prone to create the pain if none exists. We compare this to a doctor who seeks to make people sick so he can treat them.

You can certainly ask questions designed to make a prospect feel insecure. You can also share specific facts in the hope of generating fear.

The anxiety derived from these techniques is at best temporary. The client wakes up next day feeling much different. Real pain is organic. You didn't create it. You merely discovered its presence and offered to end it.

Creating pain in a prospect is not only unethical, but it's also highly ineffective.

Effective selling today is no longer about closing. Instead, it's about the opening.

It's no longer about features and benefits, mainly because your best clients don't care about them.

It's no longer about the things you say, but rather the stuff you hear.

Once you understand this reality, you are on your way to closing every prospect to whom you offer your services.

Key Take Away Points:

1. The purpose of the first meeting is to disqualify the prospect.

2. Discover what will prevent them from being an ideal client, one who wants you to handle all their financial affairs.

3. Do not hide from landmines. Discover and defuse them.

4. No emotion = no sale.

Chapter Four:
Change the Way You Operate

While computers have been around my entire career, their capabilities and the role they play in my practice changes dramatically every 36 months.

At one time, an entire office could operate with just one PC. Today, the average advisor with whom we work has at least three, usually four: a desktop at the office, a laptop for home and travel, a smartphone, and a tablet. Every employee has one. And because software gets more and more complicated, machines become obsolete so much faster.

And yet, these machines are highly underutilized by most small business owners, not just financial advisors. They are mostly typewriters, used for reading and sending an email along with a few productivity programs like QuickBooks and Excel. Oh sure, advisors know how to look up account balances and complete a financial plan, but little is done to make the advisor more productive and profitable.

Too often we fail to understand what's available.

A Day in the Life of the Automated Practice:

6:00 am: Rise to see three people ordered my Retirement Rescue Toolkit during the night. I forward the email to our fulfillment house who mails out the book, CD, and free report discussing how to rescue your 401k from taxes.

6:15 am: Receive notification that someone who ordered the kit last week has arranged a phone meeting for today at 2 pm.

9:00 am: Conduct a webinar for clients on the issue of Bitcoin. Two people register for an appointment.

10:15 am: Record and deliver podcast to over 2,000 people in my database.

11:05 am: Call from a client thanking him for the birthday card I had no idea I sent.

12:00 pm: Sent video email to client summarizing our past week's discussion.

1:22 pm: Received status report that six of my clients have shared my four-part online course on Long-Term Care.

2:11 pm: Prospect calls to schedule an appointment. Click a button that will now send him an email confirmation with map and two reminders.

3:05 pm: Client has booked his annual review through our automated reminder system.

5:00 pm: Client review via video chat with a client living in Asia.

5:20 pm: New client thanks me for the online tutorial I sent him (I did?) on how to access his account online.

Each of these tasks was completed automatically with little effort on my part.

Automation allows me to serve more clients living in more areas, cutting through more time zones while attracting new clients 24/7.

Renegade Advisors understand technology lets them break through perceived barriers.

At the basis of this type of automation is a Client Relationship Management System or CRM. Integrated with other platforms like an automated scheduler, a webinar platform, a video storage system, and a video chat program, this level of automation allows you the freedom of working virtually.

The Drug that is Facebook

About ten years ago, someone advised me to never open a Facebook account. "It will suck you in, and you'll never escape," she said.

She was half right. It has sucked me in, but I've never desired to escape.

Whether is the next Amazon or a curse from Satan himself, Facebook and social media are here to stay. At one time we wrote letters. Then phone calls. Today we text and use social media.

From a marketing perspective, Facebook has incredible value because it allows you to target your ads very narrowly.

People far more qualified than us can share with you the value of digital marketing. For starters, get a copy of Nic Kusmich's book, *Give*.

In the end, social media and automation is just another way to deliver a message. It does not change the rules of effective marketing. But there is a technical aspect that brings a list of do's and don'ts.

1. Utilize a marketing oriented client relationship management (CRM) system. We use Infusionsoft and Active Campaign. Redtail or Outlook won't do the job for you. You want a system that integrates with a landing page and then sends your clients and prospects a series of pre-written emails and downloads, and other forms of communication.

2. Hire a pro to get you started. Setting up your CRM takes expertise you probably don't have right now. You can drive a car

without knowing how it works. Same with automation.

3. Use social media advertising to promote lead magnets, NOT your firm. No one cares if you manage portfolios. What they do care about is knowing the 7 Biggest Mistakes People Make When Hiring a Financial Advisors. They'll gladly exchange their contact information for valuable materials like a book, a CD, or a DVD. We call it a "Shock & Awe" kit.

4. If you use social media to promote a workshop, you must follow up immediately. Studies show a prospect is 80% more likely to attend a seminar if you call to confirm within the first 5 minutes of when the spot was booked. Follow up with a letter (not only an email) to confirm their attendance.

5. Follow up...again and again and again. Studies show it can take as many as 18 contacts before someone is willing to buy. The CRM is built to do this, but do not abandon traditional mail. The average person receives 144 emails a day but only six pieces of physical mail.

Automation will continue to evolve at an even more rapid pace. Email once seemed revolutionary, so much so many advisors swore their clients would never use it. Renegade Advisors will embrace these changes, not by becoming experts themselves, but by hiring them to work in their business.

Key Take Away Points:

1. Acquire a marketing oriented Client Relationship Management System.

2. Develop campaigns to automate the routine activities in your firm.

3. Use social media to promote your message, not your firm. Do this with lead magnets like a "Shock & Awe" kit.

4. Hire an expert to assist you with this process.

Chapter Five:

Change the Way You Get Things Done

Here's the ultimate game-changer for your business and truly your life.

(No, we're not exaggerating!)

If you aspire to wealth, it might be useful to consider that the foundation of all wealth created in America is *systems and processes*. That's likely not surprising since everything you've read up until this point has been about how to implement systems and processes in your business.

But...

The real game changer comes when you have a system for getting *the right things done*.

If you look around at all the business owners you know – probably yourself included – you will see people trying to achieve success by repeating accidents: random acts of marketing, erratic plans, far-reaching visions and five-year goals.

They let the demands of the day guide their activities instead of knowing within a small range of variance, what the day will bring.

The Enemy of Productivity: Context Switching

Close your eyes and imagine with me for a moment...

It's Monday morning, and you've set aside some time to work on your upcoming seminar invitation.

You open Word and start to outline the important information – date, time and *location*.

What's the street address again?

No problem, you think. I'll just grab it from my email.

Switching over to Outlook, you see 3 new emails... one from your compliance office (ick!), one from a pain-in-the-rear client, and one with an intriguing subject line about increasing seminar conversions.

You're going to open that one, aren't you?

You skim the email and see a link to a video...

Click!

Now you're watching a video about some new marketing technique... but it's a little dry.

You keep the video open in the background, pop open a new window and logon to check what happened in the game you missed last night...

And before you know it, you've spent 40 minutes reading articles on an upcoming trade.

The business owner's reality is that we're surrounded by distractions and *content*. Television, radio, podcasts, social media, blogs, magazines, videos, live streaming, our phones... it's content, content, content, and if we're not careful, it can gnaw away at the minutes and hours of our lives.

However, it's not just the content that's causing us to not get anything done during our day. It's something much more sinister: context switching.

Context switching is the loss of time due to multi-tasking or switching attention from one activity to another. This phenomenon occurs because the mind must try and reacquaint itself to where you were and what you were doing.

The time and energy that it takes to get reacquainted with the project you moved away from, and are now coming back to, takes roughly 20 percent of our time.

What this means is, the more projects or goals you're trying to achieve in each day, the less actual work you'll produce!

Everything You Know About Goal Setting is a Lie

Any goal beyond 90 days is a waste of time. Those 3-year and 5-year plans? Useless. Someone shooting an arrow doesn't try to shoot a target 3 miles away!

Yes, you should have a vision for the future, but visions and tangible goals are NOT the same thing.

According to Todd Herman, a coach and business mentor and creator of the world's leading high-performance operating system for entrepreneurs and small business owners, 90 days is the horizon line framing the motivational factor we have built into our brains. Anything beyond that kills motivation and prevents taking action.

Herman first developed the 90 Day Year High Performance Operating System in the sports world, while working with Olympic and professional athletes. Hearing of its success, companies like Shell, Goldman Sachs, and Harpo Productions started reaching out to utilize it in their companies as well.

As a Certified Partner with the 90 Day Year system, I've taken his award-winning structure and translated it into an achievement engine specifically for financial advisors. Allow me to pull back the curtain enough for you to see the engine driving the success of so many entrepreneurs and business owners...

Setting Yourself Up for Success

To be a high performing advisor, a *renegade* in the industry, you need to set yourself up for success.

There are two key areas you need to focus on:

1. What the REAL drivers of success are
2. Are you performing them consistently?

Each chapter of this book represents a driver of success, a fundamental pillar, in a profitable financial advisory practice.

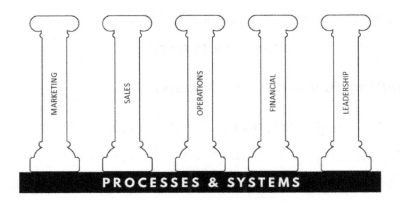

Being aware of these pillars and the processes and systems that maximize their value to your business is only the first step of the process.

The biggest hurdle is assessing where your business is *right now.*

Not where it would be if you implemented those strategies scribbled on a post-it stuck on the corner of your desk...

Not where it would be if you had new, improved staff...

You need to assess where your business is right now, and how it is currently performing in each of the 5 fundamental areas.

This process isn't always pleasant. In fact, quite often advisors will get upset or even angry when they realize that what they thought was a functional business is dysfunctional.

Build Your Achievement Plan

Once you know where you are – and where you want to go – you can map out your plan to get there. Makes sense, right?

Not so fast.

It's easy to make a list of all the things you need to do in your business.

It's not easy to act and implement.

In fact, that's the major problem with nearly every other performance-based program available today. They all focus on the bright shiny goal and the strategy, without a plan for execution.

To create a focused game plan for your next 90 days, you need to:

- Set your priorities
- Decide on your **Outcome**
- Identify the **Projects** necessary to achieve the outcome in 2-week increments
- Assign the **Processes & Tasks** necessary to make that project happen

Your Outcome Goals should tell you where you are trying to land. They are an end point and should be something very tangible, like a specific revenue number. For example, *"I will add 5 new clients by _____."*
Every Outcome Goal you set should be achieved

in the next 90 days. Remember, anything beyond 90 days is a vision, not a goal.

Your Outcome Goals are broken down into projects. In the world of business, your strategies are translated into the projects in which you've decided to invest your time, resources, money and energy.

Once you establish your Project(s), the next step is to break that project down into something you can finish in the next 2 weeks. Depending on your Outcome, you may need to work on 2 - 4 Projects to reach that Goal.

Finally, **Processes & Tasks** are things that you can schedule, assign to your staff or outsource. By identifying and assigning these **Processes & Tasks**, you are creating for yourself an ACTION plan that will put you on the road to achievement.

In the words of Todd Herman, you need to get on the field, work the plan and reap the rewards!

Outcome Goal:
Performance Based Project(s): *Broken into 2 Week Sprints*
Processes & Tasks:

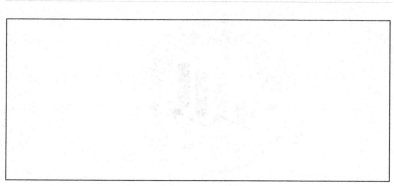

Key Take Away Points:

1. Any goal past 90 days is a waste of time.
2. Consistency is a key driver of success.
3. Implementation trumps knowledge, every time.

4. The 90 Day Year framework provides the framework that advisors need for fast growth and long-term success.

Chapter Six:

Change the Way You Earn

Twenty years ago, my practice adopted a fee-based model, believing it would provide consistent, growing revenue over time.

Admittedly, the early years were challenging. Cash flow initially took a hit, and we had to work even harder to acquire new clients to build up AUM.

Back then, most advisors were still selling commission-based products, so the switch to fee was indeed RENEGADE. Clients preferred the "pay as you go approach," and it allowed us to provide existing clients with a higher level of comprehensive service. They indeed are more valuable than new clients.

Today with $200,000,000 of assets invested through a TAMP, I couldn't be happier with that decision. Not only does our firm have a significant amount of consistent revenue arriving every quarter, but it also provides us with considerable freedom. If not for being somewhat of a workaholic, I could easily take half the year off and not see any decline in revenue.

Most advisors I meet understand how more valuable the fee-based model is, but many hesitate to make a move, fearing financial hardship during the transition. They've developed such a dependence on the front-loaded commission, mainly from annuities, they can't pull themselves away from it. It's like a highly addictive drug.

If you're over the age of 50, I get it. You're too close to the end to make a considerable change. And yet, a close friend of mine did just that at age 57. In three years, he had over $70 million in AUM.

His had two reasons for making the change. First, he was tired of having to work at a frenetic pace. He earned a lot by selling annuities, but he spent a lot as well on marketing. He was doing six to eight dinner seminars a month to fuel the addiction. His profit margin was well under 50%.

His second reason was far more pragmatic: if he didn't make the change, he feared he might be out of business.

He understood how vulnerable he was to be perceived not as an advisor, but a salesperson of product. How long would that last? How long before those products could be obtained free of commission?

From my perspective, the worst part of a commission-based practice is its lack of equity value. Other than office equipment, the practice is virtually worthless. It can't sell for any significant amount because there is no recurring income.

My friend's practice rose in value from zero to $2 million in three years just by changing how he earns.

The death of commissions has been predicted for a long time and probably will never fully materialize. There will always be people who prefer being viewed as salespeople rather than advisors. But, they'll never be able to get off the selling treadmill, they'll have no equity in their practice, and their income will likely fall as more people choose lower cost alternatives.

Other than that, it's a great way to run a business.

A Profit Focused/Fee-Based Earnings Model

What is the purpose of a small business?

Is it to provide jobs to fuel the economy?

Is it to make the world better by introducing a new technology?

Is it to fuel the passion of the owner who can't survive within the constraints of a large corporation?

Let us offer a different answer, a Renegade answer:

A Renegade Advisor knows the purpose of a small business is to create massive profits for its owner.

That's it.

Of course, what you do with those profits is up to you. You can give it to charity; you can hire more people, you can invest in new technologies. But none of these things happen if you fail to be profitable.

We know it may sound crass. It may seem insensitive; it may even look unethical.

But it's reality.

No profit, no business.

Profitable businesses tend to have a few things in common:

A Renegade Advisor knows how to maximize the revenue per customer.

In our firm, we begin by ALWAYS charging a fee for planning. And no client becomes a client without first having a plan completed. To us, recommending a strategy without first co-creating a plan with the client is akin to a doctor prescribing medicine without examining the patient. It's not only bad business, but it also borders on malpractice.

Sadly, many advisors we meet are still reluctant to do this, usually out of fear the prospect won't hire them.

They assume, falsely, that a client who won't pay them $1,500 to conduct a plan would still pay them $15,000 a year to manage their money.

Our experience is quite to the contrary. The fee not only generates more revenue for our firm, but it also serves as a filter when offering our services to clients. As detailed in Chapter 3, a profit-based practice looks to expose all objections immediately. The prospect who balks at the planning fee provides a warning of what's to come.

Prospect: No, that fee is too high for me.

Dan: I understand. Were you under the impression it would be less?

Prospect: Yes

Dan: How much less?

Prospect: I'd assumed you'd do it for free?

Dan: I see. And then how do you think I would be compensated?

Prospect: Well, if we like what you have to offer, then you would be paid.

Dan: I understand. Let me first clarify. We'll be doing a plan together, not a proposal. Much like a doctor who needs to evaluate you before prescribing medicine, we work the same way. So, we put a great deal of time and effort in our planning to ensure you get an objective analysis. That's why we charge a fee. If we didn't charge one, then you would receive a proposal. Let me ask you this. If we were to manage your portfolio, the annual fee would be 1% of its value, or about $15,000 a year. Will that be acceptable to you?

Never hide from potential objections. Face them head-on.

In addition to charging a fee for planning, the profit-based practice is always holistic. It looks to serve all the client needs, not just investments. For someone approaching retirement, that'll likely mean long-term care insurance, life insurance, tax planning, income planning, and estate planning.

A holistic approach not only offers more chances for revenue, but it also overcomes any potential objections to a fee by demonstrating the level of depth involved in the planning process.

A Renegade Advisor develops ways to collect recurring revenue from clients.

A monthly AUM fee trumps a one-time commission every time. The biggest lie you can tell yourself is that you can't afford the switch to fee-based. It's just not true. In fact, it's entirely the opposite. Of course, your FMO won't tell you that.

A Renegade Advisor continuously innovates, giving clients reasons to come back for more.

A profit-based business runs on paranoia. It continually surveys the field and finds ways to innovate out of fear competitors will take its market share. Blockbuster video, Borders Books, and America Online (AOL) lacked that fear.

The survivors evolved.

Apple was once known only for computers.

Disney made only cartoons.

Amazon sold only books.

Whatever business model you currently employ, it will eventually be obsolete. Or, it will be so much like everyone else's, you will merely be just another advisor.

The Renegade Advisor accepts the challenge of creating a total makeover every couple of years.

Even if you believe the status quo will continue for the rest of your career, there is one inevitable change you cannot control: the mortality of your clients.

Like you, someday all your clients will die. Will they die before or after you?

If you outlive them, where will their money go?

Consider your clients' children. Someday they will inherit the money you're managing. How likely will they be to hire you? Do you have a system to continue managing those assets?

If not, that paranoia should consume most of your waking thoughts. Compare the average age of your clients to yours. Who's older? If it's your clients, you should worry.

The Renegade Advisor turns this threat into a strategic advantage. He develops systems to position his practice not as a product provider but as a complete family office that essentially requires meetings with all adult children. He hosts full-day sessions with the family to explain the strategies employed for the parents and their role in the transfer process. He makes it clear if any client member has any questions or financial needs, they should quickly call him. "We're taking care of your parents, and we're happy to take care of you, too."

Renegade Advisors spend more energy keeping existing clients happy than finding new ones.

The Renegade Advisor understands it's not about a sales goal, but profit. Existing fee-based clients are far more valuable than potential new clients.

Group events and education classes bring value, but most will come from one-on-one interaction with clients where their most profound concerns are met.

Renegade Advisors don't waste money.

Great businesses reach their profit goals intentionally. They define them before the year even begins and monitor progress regularly.

It's incredible how so many advisors develop a budget for their clients but not for themselves.

The Renegade Advisor is aware of how growth can add to profitability. Nothing offers more growth potential than a practice built on AUM. But profitability can be impacted immediately by monitoring expenses and removing waste.

Key Takeaway Points:

1. Look for ways to maximize revenue per client by providing a holistic service to all clients.

2. Recurring revenue is infinitely more valuable than one-time commissions.

3. Without recurring revenue, your practice has no value for an eventual sale.

Chapter Seven:
Change the Way You Change

In the early days of Fox television, magician Val Valentino hosted a program called "Breaking the Magician's Code." Wearing a mask to protect his identity, he shared the secrets behind some of the most famous stage tricks.

As you can imagine, he irked his colleagues, many of whom later filed lawsuits.

Well, I don't have a mask, but I am going to share with you some of the secrets of the business coaching industry. I do this not to discourage you from getting help. I employ several coaches and trainers myself and mentor a number of financial advisors through my Advisor Architect program. In fact, I believe firmly that without someone working along-side of you, change is almost impossible. We naturally revert to old habits and lose focus.

You will not change by reading a book unless you have someone with you along the way. How many great athletes are self-taught? Same for actors. You can do much on your own, but a mentor will speed the process and most likely help you reach higher levels by forcing you to leave your comfort zone.

Before delving further into why you should hire a coach, let's first give you the insider's view of the industry. We're sharing this with you so that if you do hire a coach (which, for most advisors, I recommend), you do it for the right reasons and not because someone compelled you emotionally like a Nigerian prince who wants desperately to share his fortune. We also want to make sure you get your money's worth. We personally see too many cases of advisors paying exorbitant fees (often more than they can afford) for what they think will be an overnight solution to whatever ails them. Like lottery winners, it may work for some, not all.

To be a coach, you must be an authority. In some industries, this is easy. If your exercise trainer looks like The Rock, you will naturally conclude he probably knows a thing or two about toning the body. Of course, he could be the worst trainer in the world, but initially, he has earned the benefit of your doubt. By contrast, one who looks like the late John Candy would leave you rightfully dubious.

Business coaching requires a more detailed strategy in order to answer the question, "Why should I hire you?"

To develop authority, business coaches will employ a number of strategies.

Tell a compelling comeback story: You want your prospective client to see you as just like them. "If I can do it, you can do it, too." Fitness instructor Richard Simmons used to be fat. Now he's not. He'll show you how he did it. There's the business "coach" who used to owe over $450,000 because of his partner's incompetence. He paid it off in four years and will show you how he went from failed advisor to overnight success. If he can do it, so can you.

Write a book: Authors are viewed as "experts." Almost anyone can publish a book with no intellectual value and make it a categorical "#1 bestseller" on Amazon for one day. CreateSpace.com is Amazon's site for aspiring authors. Simply upload your manuscript, pick a cover, and presto! Your book is now selling on Amazon. You can print copies for less than $2.50. Then, with the help of ad firms like Celebrity Branding Agency (Nick Nanton) and Status Factory (Clint Arthur), you list your book under an obscure category within Amazon. Then arrange for 100 copies or so to be purchased by various log-in ID's and "Abracadabra," you're a best seller for a day. Of course, Paris Hilton and Kim Kardashian have also written books and got paid to do so.

Hire celebrities: B-list celebrities like Leeza Gibbons (Entertainment Tonight), Kevin Harrington (Shark Tank), and former NFL quarterback Joe Theismann will conduct a number of on-camera interviews with you to create the appearance as if you're almost as famous as they are. Again, this is the type of work done by companies like Celebrity Branding and Status Factory. The coach is not famous. He just paid money to appear to be famous by "hanging out" with the famous.

Learn from Mao: China once required its citizens to carry a little red book of their leader's most famous quotes. Authority seeking coaches often do the same thing. Their meeting rooms are full of quotes....attributed to them. My favorite one is "Control what you can control." I know for a fact my dad said that to me in 1979, not the guy selling a $68,000 coaching program.

Use Testimonials: Nothing sells better than listening to a current or former client tell you how the coach changed his life. Over and over again. Most testimonials are made in the early stage of the relationship when the euphoria is high. Those are easy to get. Less easy to obtain are testimonials a year later since results and reactions will change. Understand many of these testimonials are coerced. If you look closely, you'll notice similarities between these testimonials and the ones given by prisoners of war.

All-Star Panels: Those who succeed with the "coach" will always attend the meetings for recruiting new members. Typically, they'll wear some type of special badge to make it clear to everyone who they are. They are a walking billboard. They'll be given perks during the meeting to heighten their level of appreciation toward the coach, making it more likely they'll encourage prospective new members. This is a technique also used by Amway and The Church of Scientology.

Speak at Harvard: Again, for a fee, coaches can speak at a well-known university. That's right...they are paying the school to speak, not the other way around. The speech is recorded and then later used as an example of the "coach's authority." I know of one case where the speech was made in an empty room with applause dubbed into the video.

All of these techniques are employed at a two- or three-day "boot-camp" designed to recruit new members. Day one is usually filled with overwhelming conceptual material that emphasizes the problems you face. Day two begins with more of the same, but slowly the solutions are revealed, each of which is available to you for a price.

At a minimum, coaching services offer a set number of access hours to the coach. This can be a combination of one-on-one meetings, group meetings, monthly phone calls, emails, etc. The more private the access to the "coach," the higher the likely cost.

We've seen some programs charge as high as $45,000 in return for 29 hours of coaching time. Imagine what he/she charges if you want to go fishing with him.

Most coaching programs cost between $15,000 and $20,000 per year. Although it's easy to assume the higher price program is better, the high pricing tactic is often used by "coaches" to create perceived value. In the end, something is worth only what someone is willing to pay for it.

So, what happens during "coaching" time?

Some "coaches" will tell you the time is for whatever you want it to be, but typically they'll follow some marketing strategy framework, most of which can be found in a book by Alan Dib called <u>The One Page Marketing Plan:</u>

- Pick an affluent target market
- Find a message that resonates with them
- Deliver the message through an efficient media channel
- Develop a Lead Capture System
- Develop a Lead Nurture System
- Develop a Sales Conversion Strategy
- Deliver a World Class Experience
- Increase Lifetime Customer Value
- Stimulate Referrals

Nothing too earth-shattering, but where most small businesses fall short is not with ideas, but with implementation. It's easy to say you're going to do something. It's to do it. A good coach will move you toward implementing systems.

Sadly, too many programs focus only on marketing, thus perpetuating the myth that spending on marketing alone will automatically translate into profit. Rarely do "coaches" provide guidance in areas like results tracking, profitability management, automation, client retention, and succession planning. Most advisors I know have much larger business problems, the least of which is marketing.

But marketing draws attention, so it gets most, if not all, of the program's emphasis.

"Spend more to make more."

"If you don't have the money for my program, pull it out of your IRA."

"Put it on the credit card."

"It's not spending; it's investing. Investing in yourself is far more valuable than investing in the stock market."

These are words typically said at an FMO meeting. But "coaches" will also use them as a way to motivate you to buy their services.

The most effective programs not only offer you strategic guidance in all business areas, they also provide a great deal of "done for you" implementation at no extra cost. This can include things like a co-authored book, spreadsheets, seminar systems, social media funnels, lead magnets, and podcast services.

The least effective will charge you extra for these programs, often at a price greater than the "coach's" time. This can be a huge profit maker for the "coach" because it does not require much of his/her time. It's money in the bank.

So, who needs a coach and what should you look for when you hire one?

Good coaches offer three things: Great ideas, systems that work, and the resources to implement them. If a potential coach lacks in any of these areas, then keep reading. If not, you don't need a coach.

You need to achieve some success before hiring a coach. Yes, I know. There's that one "coach" who took a guy from selling cars to producing $1 million of AUM in three years. If that bozo can do it, so can you.

Look, people win lotteries, too. It's still not the best way to build wealth.

But hiring a coach will work best when there's already some proven talent and ability. Phil Jackson is a great coach only because he always coached teams with talent. In fact, had Jackson coached the Nets instead of the Bulls & Lakers, he'd be known as a lousy coach. Personally, I will not take on an advisor who isn't already generating $200,000 of revenue. Success comes, but rarely overnight, so patience is necessary. Success also requires capital. I'm not a fan of an advisor going broke today to become rich tomorrow. A Lotto ticket is only a buck. Coaches cost a bit more.

You must be willing to leave your comfort zone. This is not easy for everyone. If I asked you to hand $50 to a total stranger, could you do it? If not, stop reading.

Still with me? Okay, now here's what to look for before you hire a coach:

> Is he still a successful advisor? My personal trainer knows a great deal about how to get physically fit. She's built like the college basketball player she once was...20 years ago. She walks the walk. Do not hire a former advisor (or even worse a failed advisor) who tells you he has found the secret to success and now has a passion to save other advisors and their clients. Jesus saves. The rest of us seek profit hopefully by doing something we enjoy doing. Hire someone who still lives in the trenches, just like you.

> Does he provide you with all the tools (co-authored books, seminar systems, graphic design) necessary to implement his

recommended systems, or does that only come at an additional cost?

➢ Is his fee more than what you need to spend to market your business?

➢ Does he charge you more to pay him in installments versus in one lump sum? I know of one guy who charges 16% interest if you try to pay in installments. Look for a program that charges you monthly so that you pay as you go.

➢ How accessible will he be? Can you contact him outside of your scheduled calls?

Make your decision a logical one. Weigh all the factors. Fully implement. Don't let this well-intended effort go the way of your treadmill that now sits in the basement gathering dust.

The Next Step

Whenever you choose to act in ways counter to the norm, you invite criticism and even jealousy. History is full of examples of creative pioneers suffering persecution until proven right.

The renegade life can be lonely. Until, of course, people start to take notice of your success. But until then, expect doubters. Your Broker-Dealer, your RIA, your TAMP, even your friends will question you. That's okay. It's almost validation you're doing it right.

We developed our own club of like-minded renegades, people who "get you" and your way of thinking. We'd love for you to join us. Begin the process by ordering our Profit Creation Toolkit.

Get Your Free Profit Creation Toolkit

Claim Your Toolkit Online at

www.RenegadeAdvisorBook.com

or by email:

Dan@AdvisorArchitect.com

49709942R00086

Made in the USA
Middletown, DE
24 June 2019